STORIES *from* SHAKESPEARE

INTRODUCTION

William Shakespeare, born in Stratford-upon-Avon, England, in 1564, is probably the best-known playwright and poet in the world. Even those who have never seen or read his work unknowingly use Shakespeare's language, for numerous phrases have passed into common use.

The son of a prosperous glover, Shakespeare married Anne Hathaway in 1582 and had three children with her, but it was his move to London that put him on the road to fame and fortune. His plays are enormously varied, including histories, comedies and tragedies. As well as entertaining playgoers for hundreds of years, his works have inspired art, music, literature and films.

Summaries of Shakespeare's plays cannot hope to capture the brilliance of the originals, but it is hoped that the six plays outlined here may encourage readers to look at the complete texts or, better still, to see them performed.

STORIES *from* SHAKESPEARE

Retold by
NICOLA BAXTER

Illustrated by
JENNY THORNE

ARMADILLO

Published by Armadillo Books
an imprint of
Bookmart Limited
Registered Number 2372865
Trading as Bookmart Limited
Blaby Road
Wigston
Leicestershire
LE18 4SE

ISBN 1-84322-000-8

Reprinted 2003

Produced for Bookmart Limited by Nicola Baxter
PO Box 215
Framingham Earl,
Norwich Norfolk NR14 7UR

Designer: Amanda Hawkes
Production designer: Amy Barton

Printed in Singapore

CONTENTS

ALL THE WORLD'S A STAGE

In this famous speech from *As You Like It*, Shakespeare compares life to the world he knows best—that of the theatre.

All the world's a stage,
And all the men and women merely players:
They have their exits and their entrances,
And one man in his time plays many parts,
His acts being seven ages. At first the infant,
Mewling and puking in the nurse's arms.
Then the whining school-boy, with his satchel
And shining morning face, creeping like snail
Unwillingly to school. And then the lover,
Sighing like furnace, with a woeful ballad
Made to his mistress' eyebrow. Then a soldier,
Full of strange oaths, and bearded like the pard,
Jealous in honour, sudden, and quick in quarrel,
Seeking the bubble reputation
Even in the cannon's mouth. And then the justice,
In fair round belly with good capon lin'd
With eyes severe and beard of formal cut,
Full of wise saws and modern instances;
And so he plays his part. The sixth age shifts
Into the lean and slipper'd pantaloon,
With spectacles on nose and pouch on side,
His youthful hose, well sav'd, a world too wide
For his shrunk shank; and his big manly voice,
Turning again toward childish treble, pipes
And whistles in his sound. Last scene of all,
That ends this strange eventful history,
Is second childishness and mere oblivion,
Sans teeth, sans eyes, sans taste, sans every thing.

A
MIDSUMMER
NIGHT'S DREAM

Theseus, Duke of Athens, first met his bride-to-be on the field of battle, but thoughts of war soon turned to those of love. She is Hippolyta, Queen of the Amazons, and soon the noble couple will be married with much ceremony.

But elsewhere in the city, true love does not run as smoothly. Egeus, a troubled father, arrives at Theseus' court with his daughter Hermia and two young men, Demetrius and Lysander, in tow. It seems that both are in love with Hermia. Although Egeus favours Demetrius, Hermia has set her heart on Lysander and refuses to obey her father.

Egeus seems prepared to use desperate measures.

I beg the ancient privilege of Athens,
As she is mine, I may dispose of her;
Which shall be either to this gentleman
Or to her death, according to our law…

Hermia appeals to the duke, who confirms that she must obey her father or die—unless she would prefer to live as a nun for the rest of her life. Demetrius, too, tries to persuade her to do her duty. Lysander, naturally, takes a different view!

You have her father's love, Demetrius,
Let me have Hermia's; do you marry him.

Lysander also points out that Demetrius has won the heart of another young woman, a friend of Hermia's called Helena. Theseus admits that he has heard as much and would like to have a word with Demetrius about it. While discussions are taking place, Lysander and Hermia are left alone. Lysander has a plan.

Steal forth thy father's house tomorrow night;
And in the wood, a league without the town…
There will I stay for thee.

A league *was a distance of about three miles. In Elizabethan England, aristocrats loved to hunt for sport and to show off their horsemanship. The wood is also seen as a wild place where anything might happen.*

Hermia is happily agreeing when Helena comes in. The fact that Demetrius prefers Hermia to her is straining the girls' friendship. To reassure Helena, Hermia tells her of her plan to run away. Later, by herself, Helena decides to pass this information on to Demetrius. Maybe it will make him pay attention to her again.

Meanwhile, in a little house in Athens, some workmen have met to plan the entertainment they will put on during the celebrations for the duke's wedding. They are Quince the carpenter, Snug the joiner, Bottom the weaver, Flute the bellows-mender, Snout the tinker and Starveling the tailor.

The friends have decided on an ambitious presentation of *The Most Lamentable Comedy and Most Cruel Death of Pyramus and Thisbe*, a play involving high drama … and a lion! Bottom the weaver is particularly enthusiastic, wanting to play all the parts himself, but in the end he is content to be the hero, Pyramus. It is agreed that the players will all meet in the wood outside the city for secret rehearsals.

It seems that the wood is likely to be a busy place by night! It is already inhabited by a host of fairies, ruled over by Oberon the fairy king and Titania the fairy queen. Also among them is Puck, known as Robin Goodfellow. He is a mischievous sprite who likes nothing better than casting spells and causing trouble.

The humans of Athens are not the only ones to have problems. As Puck tells a passing fairy, Oberon and Titania have quarrelled.

…Oberon is passing fell and wrath,
Because that she as her attendant hath
A lovely boy stolen from an Indian king.
She never had so sweet a changeling;
And jealous Oberon would have the child
Knight of his train, to trace the forest wild;
But she perforce withholds the loved boy,
Crowns him with flowers, and makes him all her joy;
And now they never meet in grove or green,
By fountain clear, or spangled starlight sheen,
But they do square, that all their elves for fear
Creep into acorn cups and hide them there.

Oberon has plans to punish Titania for keeping the boy. He tells Puck to find a certain magical flower. When juice from it is squeezed on a person's eyelids, he or she falls in love with the next creature to appear. If Titania is spellbound in this way, she will not think twice about giving up the boy.

As night falls, Demetrius enters the wood. He is far from happy that Helena insists on following him. "I love thee not, therefore pursue me not," he tells her. Helena will not listen. "I am sick when I do look on thee," says Demetrius, doing his best to shake her off. They do not realize that Oberon is watching and listening.

When Puck returns with the magical flower, Oberon tells him exactly what he plans.

I know a bank where the wild thyme blows,
Where oxlips and the nodding violet grows,
Quite over-canopied with luscious woodbine,
With sweet musk-roses and with eglantine.
There sleeps Titania sometimes of the night…
And with the juice of this I'll streak her eyes…

But Oberon also tells Puck to take some of the juice and put it on Demetrius' eyes, so that he will fall in love with Helena after all.

Oberon finds Titania, surrounded by her sleeping attendant fairies, just as he has planned. Puck, however, not expecting to find many young Athenians wandering around the woods at night, makes a big mistake. He finds Hermia and her lover asleep beneath the trees and puts the juice on Lysander's eyes.

Unfortunately, Lysander awakes when Demetrius comes rushing past in his attempt to lose his persistent follower. The first person Lysander sees is not Hermia but Helena! At once, Lysander begins to vow his love for her. He does not mince his words:

> *Content with Hermia! No; I do repent*
> *The tedious minutes I with her have spent.*
> *Not Hermia but Helena I love.*
> *Who will not change a raven for a dove?*

Women *were not allowed to act on the Elizabethan stage. Female parts were played by men, which may have added to the comedy of some scenes.*

Helena, feeling that this is cruel mockery of her unloved state, runs off, but Lysander follows her, leaving Hermia to sleep on. When Hermia wakes shortly afterwards, she finds herself alone in the darkness.

As luck would have it, the Athenian workmen have chosen to hold their rehearsal next to the place where Titania is sleeping. It is soon clear that they have no idea at all about how to stage a play. In addition to the parts already allocated, they decide that it will be necessary for one of them to pretend to be the moon and another to take on the role of a wall.

As usual, Bottom is full of ideas, but when he disappears behind a bush between speeches, Puck sees his chance. He casts a spell over the weaver to give him the head of a donkey! When Bottom reappears, his fellow workmen run away in horror.

Titania, opening her eyes a few moments later, hears Bottom's hearty tones, as he sings to reassure himself. "What angel wakes me from my flowery bed?" she cries, and she falls immediately head-over-heels in love with the extraordinary creature. Titania summons four fairies, Peaseblossom, Cobweb, Moth and Mustardseed to attend on her beloved.

Be kind and courteous to this gentleman.
Hop in his walks and gambol in his eyes;
Feed him with apricocks and dewberries,
With purple grapes, green figs, and mulberries…
And pluck the wings from painted butterflies
To fan the moonbeams from his sleeping eyes.

Of course, Oberon is delighted when he hears what has happened, but his pleasure turns to annoyance when Demetrius hurries past, pursued by Hermia begging for news of Lysander. Oberon realizes at once that Puck has made a mistake and sends him off to find Helena, so that things can be put right. Meanwhile, Demetrius falls asleep in the glade. Oberon seizes the opportunity to squeeze some of the magic juice on his eyes.

No sooner has Demetrius closed his eyes than Lysander and Helena arrive at the same spot. Lysander is giving Helena the benefit of his most poetic speeches. But these are nothing to the flowery outpourings of Demetrius, who wakes to see Helena. "O Helen, goddess, nymph, perfect, divine!" he cries. Helena is close to tears. She is sure she is being made fun of by both men. First no one wanted her, now everyone does! "If you were civil and knew courtesy, you would not do me thus much injury," she says.

At this interesting moment, Hermia stumbles upon her friends, only to find that neither Lysander nor Demetrius pays her the slightest attention. Even Helena is not friendly. She thinks that Hermia helped to plan the trick the men are playing on her. Soon the girls are trading insults among the trees.

Oberon blames Puck for the whole sorry mess. He orders him to split the lovers up so that there is a chance of putting everything right again. Eventually, all four, unknown to each other, drop down to sleep in the same clearing. This time Puck squeezes juice on Lysander's eyes.

Meanwhile, Titania is still in love with Bottom.

> *Come, sit thee down upon this flowery bed,*
> *While I thy amiable cheeks do coy,*
> *And stick musk-roses in thy sleek smooth head,*
> *And kiss thy fair large ears, my gentle joy.*

Oberon, watching, decides that Titania's lesson has gone on long enough. With a spell, he sets her free. "My Oberon!" she cries. "What visions have I seen! Methought I was enamoured of an ass!" Puck removes Bottom's extraordinary head as dawn lights the sky.

It is not long before the sound of hunting horns heralds the arrival of Duke Theseus and Hippolyta, accompanied by Egeus and the rest of the court. Egeus is astonished to find his daughter asleep on the ground. It is, after all, the day on which she must decide her fate.

As the lovers awake, it is soon clear that all is now well. Demetrius loves Helena and is loved in return. Lysander and Hermia are as one again. The duke decides to over-rule Egeus and hold a triple wedding.

Demetrius says what all the lovers are thinking.

In ancient Athens women certainly had little say in their futures, but Shakespeare is also reflecting the fact that in Elizabethan England girls were subject to the will of their father – or an even more powerful man.

Are you sure that we're awake? It seems to me
That yet we sleep, we dream.

Only one set of people is still at odds. In Athens, the workmen are mourning Bottom—and their cancelled play. When the weaver walks in, his old self again, they are overjoyed. The show will go on! Bottom has some final words of advice.

…most dear actors, eat no onions nor garlic, for we are to utter sweet breath; and I do not doubt but to hear them say, it is a sweet comedy.

So Duke Theseus and Queen Hippolyta lead the way to the temple, where they are to be married, and Demetrius follows with Helena, Lysander with Hermia.

That evening, the happy couples celebrate in the duke's palace in Athens. They decide that the play of *Pyramus and Thisbe*, performed by Bottom and his friends, will entertain them. Of course, the play is hilarious, although the actors take their roles very seriously. Bottom, playing Pyramus, makes the most of his dramatic death scene:

Thus die I, thus, thus, thus.
Now am I dead,
Now am I fled:
My soul is in the sky:
Tongue, lose thy light!
Moon, take thy flight!
Now die, die, die, die, die.

When the party is over, and all the performers have gone, the night is left to the fairies. Titania and Oberon wish all the couples well. At last, only Puck is left. He says goodnight to the audience and reminds them that what they have seen is no more real … than a dream.

HAMLET, PRINCE OF DENMARK

Something is rotten in the state of Denmark. At midnight, in front of the royal Danish castle of Elsinore, Horatio has come to find out if reports of strange happenings are true. He does not have long to wait. A ghostly figure appears, resembling King Hamlet, who has recently died. At the crowing of a cock, the ghost disappears, but all who see it fear there is trouble to come.

Events have moved fast in the Danish court. Not only has the old king's brother Claudius become king, he has also married his brother's widow, Gertrude. Meanwhile, Fortinbras of Norway is threatening to invade.

In this turbulent setting, one figure is more uneasy than any. It is young Hamlet, son of the former king. His mother begs him to put on a happier face.

Good Hamlet, cast thy nighted colour off…
Thou know'st 'tis common; all that lives must die…

Prince Hamlet wishes to return to his studies in Wittenburg, but both his mother and his stepfather beg him to stay. The young man reluctantly agrees, but when he is alone once more, his words show the full depths of his grief.

O, that this too too solid flesh would melt,
Thaw, and resolve itself into a dew!
Or that the Everlasting had not fix'd
His canon 'gainst self-slaughter! O God! God!
How weary, stale, flat, and unprofitable,
Seem to me all the uses of this world!

Horatio is an old friend of Hamlet's. When he brings news of the ghostly sight he has seen, Hamlet decides to watch for it himself.

Meanwhile, Laertes, the son of Lord Chamberlain Polonius, is about to return to France. He takes his leave of his sister Ophelia, telling her not to trust too much in the attention that Prince Hamlet has been paying her. Polonius has many final words of wisdom for his son, finishing, at last, by saying:

This above all: to thine own self be true,
And it must follow, as the night the day,
Thou canst not then be false to any man.

Later, while the sound of merrymaking from the palace echoes through the night air, Hamlet and Horatio wait in the biting cold. The ghost appears, beckoning to Hamlet and seeming to wish to speak to him alone.

Hamlet follows the ghost and soon finds his suspicions confirmed. The ghost says that he has been killed by his own brother and asks the prince to revenge this "murder most foul". Hamlet's feelings are in turmoil. His hatred for his uncle makes his mother's actions seem even worse.

O most pernicious woman!
O villain, villain, smiling, damned villain!
…one may smile and smile, and be a villain,
At least I'm sure it may be so in Denmark.

Hamlet swears Horatio to secrecy, but his mind is still racing.

There are more things in heaven and earth,
  Horatio,
Than are dreamt of in your philosophy.
…The time is out of joint; O cursed spite…
That ever I was born to set it right!

It is not long before Hamlet's turmoil becomes known to others. Ophelia tells her father of one encounter.

My lord, as I was sewing in my closet,
Lord Hamlet, with his doublet all unbrac'd,
No hat upon his head, his stockings fouled,
Ungarter'd, and down-gyved to his ankle,
Pale as his shirt, his knees knocking each other,
And with a look so piteous in purport
As if he had been loosed out of hell
To speak of horrors,—he comes before me.

A doublet was a short, close-fitting jacket worn by men above a pair of stockings called hose. A full shirt was worn beneath the doublet, which might or might not have sleeves.

Polonius, disturbed by this news, and fearing that it shows Hamlet's passion for Ophelia is verging on madness, hurries to tell the king.

Claudius, however, is already aware of Hamlet's state of mind and suspects he knows its cause. Polonius is typically long-winded in his speech. When at last he explains about Hamlet's behaviour to Ophelia, both the king and the queen are eager to believe this may reveal the cause of Hamlet's erratic behaviour. Polonius suggests that he should eavesdrop on a conversation between the two young people.

No sooner is the plot laid than Hamlet himself appears, reading a book. His replies to questions are ambiguous. Is he really mad or toying with them all? As Polonius says, "Though this be madness, yet there is method in't."

Claudius also tries to find out more by sending two schoolfriends of Hamlet's, Rosencrantz and Guildenstern, to talk with him. Once again, Hamlet appears to be mocking them, but facets of his own dilemma shine through the word-play. "There is nothing either good or bad, but thinking makes it so," he says.

Hamlet makes it clear that he knows why Rosencrantz and Guildenstern are questioning him. He realizes that his behaviour has been causing concern. When the visitors mention that a troop of players has arrived, Hamlet's interest is caught. He welcomes the actors and privately arranges a special performance of a particular play the following night, into which he will add a speech of his own. Later, on his own, Hamlet agonizes over his lack of action and talks of his plan.

> *I'll have these players*
> *Play something like the murder of my father*
> *Before mine uncle, I'll observe his looks…*
> *…the play's the thing*
> *Wherein I'll catch the conscience of the King.*

Polonius' own plan to eavesdrop on Ophelia's next meeting with Hamlet is soon underway. Claudius and Polonius hide as Hamlet approaches. The prince is once again tortured by the situation in which he finds himself.

A soliloquy is a speech spoken by a character on his or her own. Hamlet has many famous soliloquies, which show us what the character is thinking and feeling.

> *To be, or not to be: that is the question:*
> *Whether 'tis nobler in the mind to suffer*
> *The slings and arrows of outrageous fortune,*
> *Or to take arms against a sea of troubles,*
> *And by opposing end them. To die, to sleep—*
> *No more; and by a sleep to say we end*
> *The heart-ache and the thousand natural shocks*
> *That flesh is heir to; 'tis a consummation*
> *Devoutly to be wished.*

Ophelia's meeting with the prince causes her confusion and distress. One moment he is telling her, "I did love you once." Seconds later, he asserts, "I loved you not." He leaves her feeling wretched and more worried than ever about his state of mind.

> *O, what a noble mind is here o'er-thrown!*
> *The courtier's, soldier's, scholar's, eye, tongue,*
> *   sword;*
> *Th' expectancy and rose of the fair state,*
> *The glass of fashion and the mould of form,*
> *The observ'd of all observers, quite quite down!*
> *And I, of ladies most deject and wretched,*
> *That suck'd the honey of his music vows,*
> *Now see that noble and most sovereign reason,*
> *Like sweet bells jangled out of time and harsh.*

The king, however, is not at all sure that Hamlet is mad. Having overheard everything, he feels alarmed about his own position, and decides to send Hamlet to England.

That night, the theatrical performance that Hamlet has planned with the players is presented before the court. No one who watches can be in any doubt that the subject of the play hits very close to home. A poisoner kills a king and then marries his wife. Claudius rises and stops the show, confirming once and for all in Hamlet's mind that the ghost of his father told the truth.

An arras *was a tapestry covering a wall or an alcove. In Elizabethan times, wealthy homes had tapestries for warmth and decoration.*

While the king is instructing Rosencrantz and Guildenstern to take Prince Hamlet to England, Gertrude asks to speak to her son. Old Polonius cannot resist the temptation to hide behind the arras and listen to what is said.

The queen, coming straight to the point, tells her son, "Hamlet, thou hast thy father much offended." She means Claudius, of course, but Hamlet takes it another way. "Mother," he says, "you have my father much offended."

As the argument grows heated, Gertrude becomes frightened. When she calls for help, Hamlet hears a sound behind the arras and stabs at it with his sword. He thinks he has killed Claudius at last, but finds only the body of Polonius.

> *Thou wretched, rash, intruding fool, farewell!*
> *I took thee for thy better…*

Hamlet rages at his mother, bringing her at last to a confession that she has acted wrongly. At the height of this dramatic exchange, the ghost of Hamlet's father appears to him once more, urging him to complete his revenge. Gertrude cannot see the ghost, which makes her even more sure that Hamlet is mad.

Later, the queen tells her husband what has happened. Not only has Hamlet killed Polonius, he has hidden the body and is refusing to say where it is. Now Claudius is sure. Whether he is mad or not, Hamlet is too dangerous to allow to live. The king sends with Rosencrantz and Guildenstern letters to the English court, instructing that Hamlet should be put to death on arrival.

Hamlet has gone from the royal castle, but trouble has not left with him. Ophelia, spurned by Hamlet and with her father dead, has lost her reason. News of these events has reached Laertes, who has returned from France.

Unlike Hamlet, Laertes does not hesitate to seek revenge, but Claudius persuades him that his quarrel is with Hamlet. When news comes that Hamlet's ship to England has been attacked by pirates, certainty about the prince's whereabouts is at an end.

Hard on the heels of a message that Hamlet is back on Danish soil comes the news that Ophelia has drowned herself.

There is a willow grows askant the brook,
That shows his hoar leaves in the glassy stream,
Therewith fantastic garlands did she make
Of crow-flowers, nettles, daisies, and long purples
*   …down her weedy trophies and herself*
Fell in the weeping brook. Her clothes spread wide,
And, mermaid-like, awhile they bore her up…
…Till that her garments, heavy with their drink,
Pull'd the poor wretch from her melodious lay
To muddy death.

Hamlet, unaware of what has taken place, meets up with Horatio and returns to complete his revenge. He comes across two grave-diggers, preparing a new grave. Soon, the royal party also arrives, come to bury Ophelia. Hamlet and Laertes fight but are pulled apart. It is arranged that they will have the opportunity to do battle in a more formal setting in the court.

Unknown to Hamlet, Laertes' rapier is poisoned, and so is the wine on a nearby table. The king is unable to prevent Gertrude from drinking it without giving himself away. Meanwhile, both Laertes and Hamlet are slightly wounded by the poisoned blade. As the queen falls to the ground, Hamlet realizes there is treachery afoot. He strikes at the king, knowing himself to be doomed.

Claudius dies, leaving Hamlet for only a few seconds as the King of Denmark. When the arrival of the Norwegian forces is announced, Hamlet confers the throne on young Fortinbras.

…he has my dying voice … the rest is silence.

Horatio is left to mourn.

> *Goodnight, sweet prince,*
> *And flights of angels sing thee to thy rest!*

But it is Fortinbras, the new king,
who has the final word.

> *Let four captains*
> *Bear Hamlet, like a soldier, to the stage,*
> *For he was likely, had he been put on,*
> *To have prov'd most royal.*

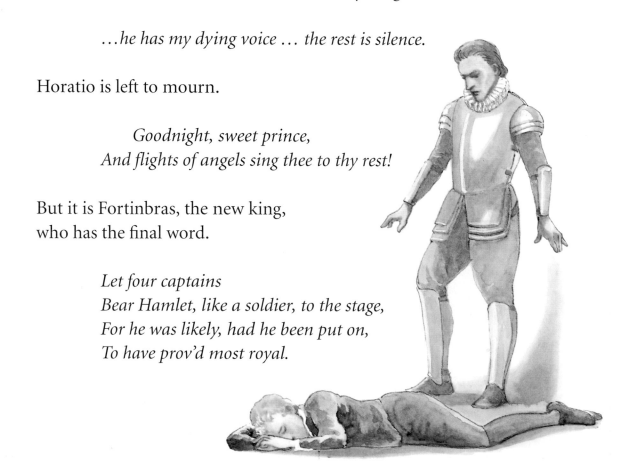

MACBETH

Lightning flashes. Thunder roars. On a desolate heath, three witches plan a fateful meeting with a man called Macbeth. The strange women talk in riddles. "Fair is foul, and foul is fair," they chant.

Meanwhile, in an army camp, King Duncan of Scotland hears news of the battle between his men and the rebel forces of Macdonwald, who has sided with the King of Norway. All has gone well for Scotland, but the victory has been hard won. Duncan hears that no sooner has his general Macbeth killed Macdonwald than the King of Norway has launched a fresh attack, this time with the help of another rebel, the Thane of Cawdor. Macbeth and Banquo, another general, have won the day for Scotland. Duncan orders Cawdor's death and expresses his intention of awarding the rebel's title to Macbeth.

Returning, wounded and exhausted, from the battle, Macbeth and Banquo encounter the three witches. "So foul and fair a day I have not seen," says Macbeth, echoing the witches' earlier words. The women greet Macbeth one by one.

All hail, Macbeth! hail to thee, thane of Glamis!
All hail, Macbeth! hail to thee, thane of Cawdor!
All hail, Macbeth, that shalt be King hereafter!

Macbeth appears strangely shocked by these words, but the witches have words for Banquo, too.

Lesser than Macbeth, and greater.
Not so happy, yet much happier.
Thou shalt get kings, though thou be none.

Before the two battle-weary men can ask questions, the witches disappear, leaving Macbeth and Banquo to wonder about what they have heard. Although Macbeth tries to laugh off the prophecies, he is stunned to receive, only a few moments later, the news that he has been made Thane of Cawdor.

Witches *were still burnt at the stake in Shakespeare's day. It was easy for someone to claim that an elderly woman had put a spell on him. Shakespeare's witches speak strangely but truly.*

Could it be that the third prophecy will also come true? Will it come to pass in any case, or must Macbeth himself do something dreadful to make sure he becomes king? As the hero leaves with Banquo, it seems he has made up his mind.

If chance will have me King,
why, chance may crown me,
Without my stir.

Meanwhile, Duncan is unaware of the turmoil in his general's mind. Speaking of the treacherous former Thane of Cawdor, he says, "There's no art to find the mind's construction in the face. He was a gentleman on whom I built an absolute trust." He does not know that the same might be said of Macbeth!

Duncan greets Macbeth and Banquo warmly and takes the opportunity to announce that his son, Malcolm, will be his heir. Furthermore, the king will spend that very night in Macbeth's castle at Inverness.

As Macbeth's wife awaits the return of her husband, she reads a message he has sent her. It tells of the witches' words. Clearly, Lady Macbeth has also dreamed of greatness, but she is not sure that her lord will seize his chance.

Yet do I fear thy nature;
It is too full of the milk of human kindness
To catch the nearest way.

When she hears that Duncan will spend the night under her roof, Lady Macbeth is clear that he must never leave the castle alive.

> *…Come, you spirits*
> *That tend on mortal thoughts, unsex me here,*
> *And fill me from the crown to the toe top-full*
> *Of direst cruelty!*

Although Macbeth has ridden on ahead, there is little time for discussion before King Duncan arrives. The King's first words once again underline how unaware he is of the danger he is in.

> *This castle hath a pleasnt seat; the air*
> *Nimbly and sweetly recommends itself*
> *Unto our gentle senses.*

Later, as the King dines by torchlight, Macbeth agonizes about the dreadful deed he is considering.

> *He's here in double trust:*
> *First, as I am his kinsman and his subject,*
> *…then, as his host,*
> *Who should against his murderer shut the door,*
> *Not bear the knife myself.*

Lady Macbeth, seeing her husband's indecision, speaks words of shocking violence to urge him to kill the king.

> *I have given suck, and know*
> *How tender 't is to love the babe that milks me;*
> *I would, while it was smiling in my face,*
> *Have pluck'd my nipple from his boneless gums*
> *And dash'd the brains out, had I so sworn as you*
> *Have done to this.*

The couple plan to stab Duncan as he sleeps, then leave the bloody daggers by the king's sleeping servants so that they will take the blame. In the meantime, a smiling host and hostess return to the banquet:

> *False face must hide what the false heart doth know.*

That night, when the King has gone to bed, Macbeth waits for the castle to be quiet. His overwrought imagination plays strange tricks on him.

> *Is this a dagger which I see*
> *before me,*
> *The handle toward my*
> *hand?*
> *Come, let me clutch thee.*
> *I have thee not, and yet I see*
> *thee still.*

Later, Lady Macbeth waits for her husband to come out of Duncan's chamber. She would, she says, have done the deed herself, but the sleeping king reminded her of her father. Macbeth emerges, his hands red with blood. Now it is he who loses his nerve. He does not want to return to the chamber to smear the sleeping servants with blood. Lady Macbeth seizes the daggers and goes in herself.

Just at this moment, the quiet of the castle is shattered by a thunderous knocking at the gates. The porter lets in Macduff and Lennox, who have been asked to rouse the king early so that he can go on his way. It is Macduff who discovers Duncan's body. In the confusion that follows, Macbeth cunningly kills the king's two servants so that they cannot deny the murder. When asked why he did so, he plays his part well.

Who can be wise, amaz'd, temp'rate and furious,
Loyal and neutral, in a moment? No man.

Donalbain and Malcolm, Duncan's sons, realizing that they too may be in danger, decide to flee to Ireland and England.

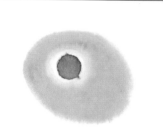

Omens *and portents often feature in Shakespeare's plays. When nature itself seems to mirror the dreadful deeds of men, they appear to be even more significant and, ultimately, tragic.*

To some onlookers, it seems that events outside the castle mirror the unnatural events within. Daylight is overtaken by darkness; wild animals act strangely; and Duncan's horses are said to have attacked each other.

With Duncan's sons gone, Macbeth is the obvious candidate for the throne. Many noblemen, including Banquo, fear that he came by it unlawfully, but now that Macbeth is in power, who dares to challenge him? He publicly blames Duncan's sons for the murder.

Yet Macbeth does not feel secure. In particular, he fears Banquo, who was present when the witches made their prophecy.

To be thus is nothing;
But to be safely thus. Our fears in
Banquo
Stick deep; and in his royalty of nature
Reigns that which would be fear'd.

The king also remembers that it is Banquo's descendants, not his own, who are to be kings. Once again, Macbeth decides there is only one thing to be done. He summons two murderers and orders them to ensure that Banquo never returns from his ride that afternoon.

But even when planning the darkest deeds, Macbeth's inner struggles show on his face. Lady Macbeth speaks firmly.

> *Things without all remedy*
> *Should be without regard; what's done is done…*
> *Gentle my lord, sleek o'er your rugged looks;*
> *Be bright and jovial among your guests tonight.*

Meanwhile, the murderers, joined by a third whom Macbeth has sent to make trebly sure the deed is done, confront Banquo and his son Fleance in open countryside. Banquo is killed, but he is able to warn the boy in time, and Fleance escapes.

That night, Macbeth and his wife host a banquet. Many Scottish lords are there. As the guests take their seats, Macbeth spots one of the murderers at the door. He learns of Banquo's death and Fleance's escape and returns to the feast with a troubled mind.

But when Macbeth reaches the top table, all the places seem to be occupied, although many bid him be seated. To the king's horror, the blood-spattered ghost of Banquo appears to him at the table. This time, Macbeth cannot hide his horror from all present.

Lady Macbeth tries to cover for him.

Sit, worthy friends; my lord is often thus,
And hath been from his youth. Pray you, keep seat;
The fit is momentary; upon a thought
He will again be well.

Indeed, Macbeth does recover his composure when the ghost disappears, but no sooner has he done so than the spectre appears again. Lady Macbeth hurries the guests away, afraid that her husband will say too much in his fearful state. Meanwhile, Macbeth has decided what he must do. He will visit the witches again to find out the worst, for there is no way back now.

I am in blood
Stepp'd in so far that, should I wade no more,
Returning were as tedious as go o'er.

Among the Scottish lords, there is much whispering about the king they now call a tyrant. Many suspect his part in the deaths of Duncan and Banquo. Noble Macduff has gone to the English court to join Malcolm, who is raising an army in order to seize back the throne of Scotland.

In a firelit cavern, Macbeth once more encounters the witches. Once again, Macbeth receives three messages, this time from three apparitions. First, a head in full armour tells him, "Macbeth! Macbeth! beware Macduff…". Then a child covered in blood tells him to be "bloody, bold and resolute … for none of woman born shall harm Macbeth". Finally, the spectre of a child in a crown, holding a tree, gives the news that "Macbeth shall never vanquish'd be until Great Birnam wood to high Dunsinane hill shall come against him".

It seems that Macbeth is safe, but the witches have more to show. An apparition of eight kings followed by Banquo implies that Macbeth's heirs will not reign after him.

Leaving the cave, Macbeth's first thought is to kill Macduff. When he hears that the lord has left for England, he orders that Macduff's wife and children shall be put to the sword instead.

At the English court, news of what has happened to his family fills Macduff and Malcolm with a new fervour to overthrow Macbeth. Edward, King of England, has lent them ten thousand men. They are ready to march on Scotland.

But at the castle of Dunsinane, Lady Macbeth, who once pushed Macbeth towards his fate, has herself broken down under the intolerable strain.

Sleepwalking, she rubs her hands together, as if trying to wash blood from them, and talks wildly of Banquo and Macduff's dead wife. Those listening can no longer be in any doubt about what is on her conscience.

As the English forces approach Birnam Wood, near Dunsinane, Macbeth feels he has nothing to fear.

> *I'll fight till from my bones*
> *my flesh be hack'd.*
> *Bring me my armour.*

Yet news that Lady Macbeth is dead leads Macbeth to face the hopeless bleakness of his life.

> *Tomorrow, and tomorrow, and tomorrow,*
> *Creeps in this petty pace from day to day*
> *To the last syllable of recorded time;*
> *And all our yesterdays have lighted fools*
> *The way to dusty death. Out, out, brief candle!*
> *Life's but a walking shadow, a poor player*
> *That struts and frets his hour upon the stage*
> *And then is heard no more. It is a tale*
> *Told by an idiot, full of sound and fury,*
> *Signifying nothing.*

At this desperate moment, things get worse for Macbeth. A messenger brings the news that Birnam Wood does indeed appear to be moving towards Dunsinane. The soldiers are carrying branches so that their approach and numbers are obscured from the castle. At this moment, we are reminded of Macbeth as he first appeared—a fearless general, leading by example.

> *Blow, wind! come, wrack!*
> *At least we'll die with harness on our back.*

The battle rages with the advantage soon going to the English force, yet Macbeth is determined to fight on. Only when challenged by Macduff does he pause, knowing how much he has already wounded the man. For if Macbeth cannot be slain by a man born of a woman, how can Macduff possibly triumph? Macduff himself has the answer, and it strikes Macbeth like a death blow.

Despair thy charm;
And let the angel whom thou still hast serv'd
Tell thee, Macduff was from his mother's womb
Untimely ripp'd.

Realizing that he has nothing to lose, Macbeth plunges forward.

Lay on, Macduff,
And damn'd be him that first cries,
*   "Hold, enough!"*

The final moments of Macbeth's life happen offstage. Macduff returns, carrying the head of the tyrant and hails Malcolm as King of Scotland. The tragedy of Macbeth is at an end.

ROMEO
AND
JULIET

In the Italian city of Verona, two families bear an ancient grudge. In the streets, the servants of the Montague and Capulet families squabble and scuffle. When Benvolio, a nephew to the head of the Montague family, and Tybalt, a nephew to Lady Capulet, come across each other, they are soon using their swords. Only the arrival of Prince Escalus restores the peace. He warns the heads of both families that he cannot tolerate this feud.

> *If ever you disturb our streets again*
> *Your lives shall pay the forfeit of the peace.*

The crowds disperse, leaving the Montagues to talk to Benvolio. Lady Montague asks if Benvolio has seen her son Romeo. It seems he has been acting strangely of late.

As Romeo approaches, Benvolio undertakes to find out what the matter is. It is soon clear that Romeo is in love, but Rosaline, the object of his affections does not return them. Benvolio's advice is matter of fact: "Forget to think of her … examine other beauties."

Meanwhile, the head of the Capulet family is also talking of love. Count Paris, a young nobleman related to Prince Escalus, is eager to marry Capulet's daughter Juliet, who is barely fourteen. Although Capulet would prefer to delay, he tells Paris that Juliet's own feelings will affect his decision. Tonight's feast will give Paris an opportunity to woo Juliet.

High-born ladies in *Shakespeare's time rarely breastfed their children. Often a wet-nurse, who, like Juliet's nurse, had lost her own baby, was used. Juliet's nurse has become almost part of the family.*

In the Capulet house, Lady Capulet decides to have a word with her daughter. Juliet's talkative nurse makes sure she is also present for this most interesting conversation. Lady Capulet comes straight to the point.

> *…think of marriage now; younger than you*
> *Here in Verona, ladies of esteem,*
> *Are made already mothers.*

Juliet shows herself to be an obedient daughter. She promises to look favourably upon Paris but to be guided by her mother.

Outside, Romeo, Benvolio and Romeo's friend Mercutio are preparing to gatecrash the party. As it is a masked ball, they stand some chance of success, but they could be in serious trouble if they are discovered. Romeo feels a sense of foreboding that perhaps is a warning of the tragedy to come.

Inside, all is merriment and dancing. Across the crowded room, Romeo sees a girl who makes all thought of Rosaline fly out of his head and his heart.

> *O, she doth teach the torches to burn bright!*
> *…Did my heart love till now? Forswear it, sight!*
> *For I ne'er saw true beauty till this night.*

It is, of course, Juliet. Unfortunately, Romeo's raptures have drawn the attention of Tybalt, who suspects from his voice that Romeo is a Montague. Tybalt is all for challenging the interloper, but old Capulet, recognizing the man behind the mask, is keen to keep the peace. Tybalt is unhappy, but Romeo meanwhile has taken the opportunity to address Juliet directly. It is not long before she is as smitten as her admirer. As Romeo leaves, Juliet, learning his name at last, realizes how difficult their situation is.

> *My only love sprung from my only hate!*
> *Too early seen unknown, and known too late!*

Later that night, Romeo climbs secretly into the Capulets' orchard. When Juliet appears on her balcony, he is overwhelmed by love for her. Juliet speaks, and her feelings are soon clear:

O Romeo, Romeo! wherefore art thou Romeo?
Deny thy father and refuse thy name;
Or, if you wilt not, be but sworn my
love,
And I'll no longer be a Capulet...
What's in a name?
That which we call a rose
By any other word would smell as
sweet...

Juliet's famous speech *is often misunderstood. "Wherefore" does not mean "where" but "why". Juliet is asking why the man she loves belongs to a rival family.*

Romeo makes himself known to Juliet, and the lovers talk until dawn. If Romeo's intentions are honourable, Juliet says, she will meet him the next day and be secretly married to him. Reluctantly, the lovers part.

Good-night, good-night! Parting is such sweet sorrow...

In the early morning, Friar Lawrence is gathering herbs when Romeo greets him. The friar guesses that Romeo has been up all night. When he hears that Juliet, not Rosaline, is now Romeo's love, the friar sees a chance to end the feud between the Capulets and the Montagues once and for all.

In the streets of Verona, Mercutio and Benvolio are still looking for their missing friend. Tybalt has sent a formal challenge to Romeo's house.

When Romeo turns up at last, the friends engage in joking banter until they come across Juliet's nurse with her servant. It seems she has a message for Romeo. Amid the high-spirited young men, the nurse gives as good as she gets, and she warns Romeo not to trifle with her charge's affections. But in her heart, the nurse is on the side of young love. She promises to tell Juliet to be at Friar Lawrence's cell that afternoon, where she and Romeo can be married.

In the orchard of her father's house, Juliet waits impatiently for the nurse to return. When the good woman arrives, she teases Juliet by holding back her news. At last, however, all is clear. The marriage will go ahead.

It is a hot day. In the streets of Verona, Mercutio and Benvolio unfortunately come across Tybalt and others of the Capulet camp. As insults are exchanged, the arrival of Romeo, already secretly married to Juliet, heats the situation further. Tybalt does not beat about the bush:

Romeo, the love I bear thee can afford
No better term than this: thou art a villain.

Romeo's soft answers to insults exasperate Mercutio, however. He draws his sword, and Tybalt does the same. In vain, Romeo tries to stop them, but his efforts only succeed in hindering Mercutio. With Romeo in the way, Mercutio receives a fatal wound.

With the death of his friend, Romeo runs out of choices. He fights with Tybalt and kills him. Now, under the Prince's edict, Romeo is under a death sentence. He flees as the discovery of Tybalt's bloody body is made.

Although Mercutio speaks up for Romeo when Prince Escalus and the heads of the Montague and Capulet families gather, the prince has had enough of civil strife.

…Let Romeo hence in haste,
Else, when he's found, that hour is his last.

By evening, Juliet, unaware of the events of the afternoon, is eager for the arrival of Romeo. The nurse's news of Tybalt's death leaves the girl in a whirl of emotions. She was fond of Tybalt, but her loyalty to her new husband is stronger. The thought that Romeo has been banished by the Prince is dreadful to her.

Meanwhile, Romeo has sought refuge at Friar Lawrence's cell. Juliet's nurse, finding him there, sees that he is just as distraught as her young mistress. Friar Lawrence tells Romeo to go to Juliet but to leave before dawn for Mantua. In the young man's absence, news of the marriage can be made known and, perhaps, all can be reconciled before his return.

Yet even while the young lovers are secretly meeting in Juliet's chamber, Old Capulet and his wife are planning her marriage to Paris. It is fixed to take place in three days' time.

As dawn draws near, Romeo and Juliet prepare to part on Juliet's balcony. For Juliet the time has come too soon.

Wilt thou be gone? It is not yet near day:
It was the nightingale, and not the lark,
That pierc'd the fearful hollow of thine ear;
Nightly she sings on yond pomegranate-tree.
Believe me, love, it was the nightingale.

The arrival of the nurse, with news that Juliet's mother is on her way, makes the parting more urgent. When Juliet hears that her marriage to Paris has been arranged, she resolutely refuses. Her father arrives to give his weight to the argument, but Juliet's refusal angers him greatly. In the end, he tells his daughter that she will marry Paris or be cast out of her home and family for ever. All Juliet can think of is to consult Friar Lawrence, but already she is considering more desperate measures.

The good friar sees a possible way forward.

> *...go home, be merry, give consent*
> *To marry Paris...To-morrow night...*
> *Take thou this vial, being then in bed,*
> *And this distilling liquor drink thou off;*
> *When presently through all thy veins shall run*
> *A cold and drowsy humour: for no pulse*
> *Shall keep his native progress, but surcease;*
> *No warmth, no breath, shall testify thou livest...*

Thinking she is dead, Juliet's parents will place her in the family vault. Meanwhile, Friar Lawrence will summon Romeo, who will take her back to Mantua. Juliet eagerly agrees to the plan.

In the Capulet house, all is hustle and bustle for the wedding. Juliet's parents are delighted by her apparent change of mind. Once again, no one has any idea of what is going on in Juliet's room. When the nurse goes to wake her in the morning, she finds her charge lifeless on the bed.

Great is the grief in the Capulet household, although Friar Lawrence, knowing more, tries to calm the family. Juliet is carried to the Capulet tomb.

In Mantua, Romeo hears news of Juliet's death before the message from Friar Lawrence reaches him. He feels that there is no point in living. Buying a dram of poison, he sets off for Juliet's grave.

As soon as he hears his message has not arrived, Friar Lawrence, too, hurries to Juliet's tomb, to release her when she awakes.

It is night when Romeo arrives at his beloved's resting place. Unfortunately, Paris has also chosen this moment to pay his respects. Both men are distraught. They fight, and Paris is killed.

Inside the tomb, Romeo kisses Juliet one last time and drinks the poison he has brought. Friar Lawrence arrives too late. As he looks into the tomb, Juliet awakes at last to see the corpses of Paris, Romeo and her kinsman Tybalt, who has been placed in the family tomb, all lying nearby.

At the sound of someone approaching, however, the friar flees, urging Juliet to follow him. But Juliet wants nothing more from life. Seizing Romeo's dagger, she stabs herself and falls beside him.

Summoned by the watchmen, Prince Escalus is first upon the tragic scene, closely followed by the Capulets and the Montagues. The two families are reconciled at last—but at an enormous price.

…never was a story of more woe
Than this of Juliet and her Romeo.

TWELFTH NIGHT

Orsino, Duke of Illyria, is in love, and everyone in the court knows that the lady Olivia is the object of his affections, as he waits for news from her.

If music be the food of love, play on!
Give me excess of it…

Unfortunately, Olivia has recently lost her brother and has vowed not to show her face to the world for seven years. The duke, however, seems determined to wallow in his hopeless passion.

Meanwhile, on the coast of Illyria, a sea captain and some of his crew help a young woman called Viola to the shore. They have all been shipwrecked. Viola's greatest concern is for her brother Sebastian, who is missing and feared drowned.

The captain knows Illyria well and tells Viola about the country. Even he has heard of Orsino's feelings for Olivia! Viola is anxious not to present herself to the world until she feels ready. She asks the captain to help her disguise herself as a boy so that she can seek employment at the duke's court.

In the lady Olivia's house, all is not as sober as might be expected. Her uncle, Sir Toby Belch, and his dim-witted friend, Sir Andrew Aguecheek, are in residence, exasperating and amusing Maria, Olivia's maidservant. Sir Toby, looking for a comfortable life, is hoping that his friend might marry his niece—and meanwhile making free with Sir Andrew's cash.

In the court of Duke Orsino, Viola has found employment and favour. She calls herself Cesario. It is not long before Orsino is asking Cesario to carry messages to Olivia. However, matters are infinitely more complicated than he knows. Not only is Cesario really a woman, but she is also in love with her employer!

*A **fool**, also known as a clown, was often kept in a wealthy household to entertain and amuse. In Shakespeare's plays, fools often speak truths in the form of jokes and riddles.*

Viola arrives at Olivia's household, where the lady's fool, Feste, has been entertaining her with witty conversation. Malvolio, Olivia's steward, is less than impressed by this, but his lack of humour does not find favour with Olivia. "O, you are sick of self-love, Malvolio," she says.

Reports of Viola's persistence eventually intrigue Olivia, who veils herself and bids the young man speak. Viola (dressed as Cesario) displays a mixture of intelligence, sympathy and wit that engages the lady far more than Orsino's overblown professions of love have ever done.

When Viola at last sees Olivia's face, she is also seeing the face of her rival.

> 'Tis beauty truly blent, whose red and white
> Nature's own sweet and cunning hand laid on.
> Lady, you are the cruell'st she alive,
> If you will lead these graces to the grave
> And leave the world no copy.

Olivia still wants to hear no more of the Duke, but she already feels more than an interest in Cesario.

> Get you to your lord.
> I cannot love him. Let him send no more,—
> Unless, perchance, you come to me again
> To tell me how he takes it.

When Viola leaves, Olivia sends Malvolio after her with a ring, on the pretence that the messenger has dropped it. Viola at once guesses what this means.

My master loves her dearly;
And I, poor monster, fond as much on him;
And she, mistaken, seems to dote on me.
What will become of this?

At this complicated point, we learn that Sebastian, Viola's twin brother, has also escaped death and is on his way to Orsino's court. With him is Antonio, despite the fact that this loyal friend has reason to fear enemies he has made at the court.

Disguises *obviously delighted Shakespeare and his audiences. It was, perhaps, easier than it is today for Sebastian and Viola to seem like twins on the Elizabethan stage, as both of them were played by men!*

That night, Sir Toby and his cronies drink and sing at Olivia's home. Malvolio comes to remonstrate with them.

Sir Toby … My lady bid me tell you … If you can
separate yourself and your misdemeanours, you are
welcome to the house; if not, an it would please you to take
leave of her, she is very willing to bid you farewell.

The revellers are disgusted by Malvolio's pomposity and at once begin to plan how to bring about the steward's downfall. They decide to leave letters around for him to find, hinting that the lady Olivia is in love with him.

Orsino is also up late, sighing and talking of love with the youth he knows as Cesario. When Viola protests that women feel such emotions as strongly as men, she is forced to speak in riddles:

> *My father had a daughter lov'd a man,*
> *As it might be, perhaps, were I a woman,*
> *I should your lordship…*
> *She never told her love,*
> *But let concealment, like a worm i' the bud,*
> *Feed on her damask cheek. She pin'd in thought,*
> *And with a green and yellow melancholy*
> *She sat, like Patience on a monument,*
> *Smiling at grief.*

Moved, but not really knowing why, Orsino gives Viola a jewel to take to Olivia.

At Olivia's house, the plot to ensnare Malvolio is well underway. Maria has faked Olivia's handwriting in a letter full of mysterious hints that she is in love. Of couse, Malvolio is quick to see himself as the cause of her feelings. In particular the letter mentions certain yellow stockings and a wish to see them "ever cross-gartered", as well as advising the reader to "be opposite with a kinsman, surly with servants".

So self-opinionated is Malvolio that he does not notice Olivia's obvious attraction to the messenger from the duke. When Viola calls again, Olivia is frank about her feelings. Viola is as truthful as she can be in the circumstances.

By innocence I swear, and by my youth,
I have one heart, one bosom, and one truth,
And that no woman has; nor never none
Shall mistress be of it, save I alone.

Sir Andrew Aguecheek, for all his foolishness, is more perceptive than Malvolio. "I saw your niece do more favours to the Count's serving-man than ever she bestowed upon me," he tells Sir Toby. Needing Sir Andrew's money, Sir Toby attempts to persuade him that Olivia's actions were merely to inflame the knight further! Sir Andrew decides to write a letter to Cesario, challenging him to a duel.

Nearby, Sebastian and Antonio decide to split up as Antonio does not wish to appear in public in case he is recognized. Sebastian agrees to look after his purse until they meet up that evening.

The astonishing behaviour of Malvolio has come to Olivia's attention. Not only is he wearing yellow stockings with cross-gartering, a fashion she hates, but he is acting very strangely. Only the arrival of Viola draws Olivia's attention away. She tells Sir Toby to take care of Malvolio, convinced that he is losing his mind.

There is also the matter of Sir Andrew's challenge to sort out. The knight words it so mildly that Sir Toby feels Cesario will not take it seriously. He prepares a more robust challenge himself. On receiving the challenge, Viola is horrified. She has no idea how to fight a duel! Sir Toby's tales of Sir Andrew's violent temper unnerve her even more. The trickster Sir Toby meanwhile regales Sir Andrew with news of Cesario's brilliance with the sword. With much trembling on both sides, the two prepare to fight.

It is at this moment that Antonio happens by. He immediately dashes to the aid of the youth he believes to be Sebastian. Before damage can be done, officers arrive and arrest Antonio, but his situation distresses him far less than Viola's refusal to recognize him. She also, of course, denies having his purse.

As Antonio is dragged away, he calls upon his friend Sebastian. Suddenly, Viola is filled with hope that her brother might be alive.

Sebastian, too, finds his identity mistaken, for Feste the fool comes across him, closely followed

by Sir Toby and Sir Andrew.
Thinking Sebastian is Cesario,
Sir Toby urges them to
continue fighting. This time, it
is a very different story, and Sir
Andrew has much to fear.
Luckily, Olivia arrives and
breaks up the fight. She leads
the astonished Sebastian back
to her house, professing her
love for him. Sebastian is hardly
reluctant. "If it be thus to dream,"
he says, "still let me sleep!"

 Sir Toby's mischief is not yet ended. He has shut
Malvolio up in a little, dark room. By the time
Sir Toby has finished tricking and goading, even
Malvolio believes himself to be mad.

While her varied household is
occupied, Olivia is delighted to
find that her feelings for Cesario
(actually, of course, Sebastian)
are returned with passion.
Sebastian is only too ready to
agree to accompany her to a
priest for a secret marriage.

Orsino, arriving in person at
Olivia's house, encounters
Antonio being brought to the
court by the officers. Viola

identifies Antonio as the man who saved her from her duel with Sir Andrew Aguecheek but, of course, continues to deny that she holds his purse.

When Olivia arrives and addresses Cesario/Viola as her lord and husband, confusion reigns, especially when the priest enters and confirms that he has (as he thinks) married the pair. The duke's sense of betrayal is interrupted by the arrival of Sir Andrew, claiming that he and Sir Toby have both been wounded by Cesario. As they are led away to be tended to, the arrival of Sebastian brings about the resolution of the situation.

One face, one voice, one habit, and two persons…

The duke is astonished as he looks from Viola to her brother. Soon, all is clear, and Sebastian and Viola are overjoyed to meet again, while Olivia happily finds her new husband has had no change of heart.

A plaintive letter from Malvolio is delivered to Olivia, showing that he is not mad but badly used. When Malvolio himself is brought forward, the whole trick of the letter is revealed.

Now all that is needed is for Viola to dress again as a woman. All, it seems, will end happily for her as well. Orsino declares:

Cesario, come;
For so you shall be, while you are a man;
But when in other habits you are seen,
Orsino's mistress and his fancy's queen.

As everyone departs, it is left to Feste the fool to end the play with a gently poignant song.

When that I was and a little tiny boy,
    With hey, ho, the wind and the rain,
A foolish thing was but a toy,
    For the rain it raineth every day.

But when I came to man's estate,
    With hey, ho, the wind and the rain,
'Gainst knaves and thieves men shut their gate,
    For the rain it raineth every day.

But when I came, alas! to wive,
    With hey, ho, the wind and the rain,
By swaggering could I never thrive,
    For the rain it raineth every day.

But when I came unto my beds,
    With hey, ho, the wind and the rain,
With toss-pots still had drunken heads,
    For the rain it raineth every day.

A great while ago the world begun,
    With hey, ho, the wind and the rain,
But that's all one, our play is done,
    And we'll strive to please you every day.

ANTONY
AND
CLEOPATRA

In the Egyptian city of Alexandria, all talk is of the love affair between Cleopatra, the queen, and Mark Antony, a Roman general and triumvir. Antony seems to have forgotten his duty and his wife at home. And Cleopatra, a fascinating and beautiful woman, is cleverly doing her best to keep him by her side.

When a messenger brings news that Rome's enemies are gathering and Antony's wife is dead, even the lovesick Roman feels a pang of guilt.

> *I must from this enchanting queen break off:*
> *Ten thousand harms, more than the ills I know,*
> *My idleness doth hatch.*

Cleopatra does her best to make Antony stay, but when she sees that his mind is made up, she wishes him well.

> *…your honour calls you hence;*
> *Therefore be deaf to my unpitied folly,*
> *And all the gods go with you!*

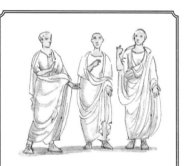

A triumvir *was one of the three men who ruled the Roman empire at this period. They had huge power and responsibilities. The other two triumvirs were Octavius Caesar and Lepidus.*

Meanwhile, back in Rome, Octavius Caesar and Lepidus, Antony's fellow triumvirs, are worried not only by the gossip about Antony but also by the news that Pompey is preparing to attack Rome by sea. Now more than ever they need Antony's brilliance as a general to lead their armies against the enemies of Rome. But will Antony come?

Pompey is concerned to hear that Antony is, in fact, on his way back to Rome. He had hoped not to have to fight against such a great leader. But he comforts himself with the fact that the Romans must be truly worried by his threat if they have to call for Mark Antony.

The meeting of Octavius and Antony is predictably tense, but Antony apologises for his behaviour. Agrippa seizes the opportunity to suggest an even closer bond between the two men. Antony is now a widower, and Octavius has an unmarried sister, Octavia… To calm the situation, Antony agrees to the match.

As Octavius leads Antony off to meet his wife-to-be, Enobarbus, Antony's righthand man, takes the opportunity to catch up with old friends in Rome. Naturally, they are anxious to hear all the latest gossip from Egypt and to find out if Cleopatra is really as amazing as they have heard.

Enobarbus is a soldier, but he becomes a poet as he describes the first time that Antony and Cleopatra met.

The barge she sat in, like a burnish'd throne,
Burn'd on the water: the poop was beaten gold;
Purple the sails, and so perfumed that
The winds were love-sick with them: the oars
*   were silver,*
Which to the tune of flutes kept stroke…

It seems that Cleopatra herself was no less breathtaking.

> *…she did lie*
> *In her pavilion—cloth-of-gold of tissue—*
> *O'er-picturing that Venus where we see*
> *The fancy outwork nature. On each side her*
> *Stood pretty dimpled boys, like smiling Cupids,*
> *With divers-colour'd fans, whose wind did seem*
> *To glow the delicate cheeks which they did cool,*
> *And what they undid did.*

When his friends suggest that Antony must give up Cleopatra now, Enobarbus shakes his head.

> *Never; he will not.*
> *Age cannot wither her, nor custom stale*
> *Her infinite variety.*

Venus *was the Roman goddess of love. In Greek legends, her name was Aphrodite, and her beauty brought about the terrible war of Troy. Cleopatra, too, will be the cause of bloodshed.*

Later, as Antony prepares to leave Caesar's house, he meets an Egyptian soothsayer—a man who claims to see into the future. He warns Antony that Caesar will always triumph in any contest between them.

Although, seconds before, he has promised Octavia that his past behaviour is over, Antony decides to return to Egypt as soon as he can.

Meanwhile, in Egypt, Cleopatra is restless. When a messenger arrives from Rome, she is desperate to hear that Antony is well. The news that he is married is a huge blow, yet within minutes she is plotting how to regain his love.

Near Misenum, the triumvirs meet Pompey to try to avoid the war that threatens. Thanks to Caesar's diplomacy, agreement is reached and a great feast is held on board Pompey's flagship. As the wine flows, the difference in character between sober Caesar and life-loving Antony is all too clear. When Antony leaves for Athens with his new bride in the morning, Octavius is far from sure that her future will be happy.

In Alexandria, Cleopatra finds out details about her rival and feels more confident. "All may be well enough," she tells her maids Iris and Charmian.

The truce between Caesar and Antony does not last long. When, in Athens, Antony hears that Caesar has, after all, waged war on Pompey, he prepares to take up arms against his new brother-in-law. Octavia, torn between the brother she loves and her new husband, begs for the chance to act as go-between. Antony is only too happy to let her go.

As Enobarbus later hears, there is other news from Rome. Octavius has imprisoned Lepidus and taken all the power himself. With Pompey dead, Antony and Octavius are on a collision course, especially as, even before his new wife has reached Rome, Antony is already in Egypt with Cleopatra.

A queen with Cleopatra's qualities would have seemed even more exotic in Shakespeare's England. Elizabeth I, the Virgin Queen, had not long been dead when this play was first performed.

Octavius does not hesitate to tell his sister what has happened. He assures her that the injustice that has been done to her will be revenged.

War is inevitable now, and back in Egypt Cleopatra is determined to play a full part. Enobarbus begs her to withdraw.

> *Your presence needs must puzzle Antony;*
> *Take from his heart, take from his brain,*
> *   from's time,*
> *What should not then be spar'd.*

But Cleopatra's mind is made up. "I will not stay behind," she says.

News of the approach of Octavius' fleet makes Antony rash. He decides to fight by sea, although his land army is much stronger. Enobarbus, an experienced soldier, begs him to reconsider.

Most worthy sir, you therein throw away
The absolute soldiership you have by land … and
Give yourself merely to chance and hazard,
From firm security.

But Antony will not be advised. All too soon, an appalled Enobarbus hears that the sea battle has been a complete fiasco. It seems that Cleopatra turned her ships for home, and Antony, regardless of the state of the fight, followed her. "I never saw an action of such shame," reports a soldier who was there.

Unsurprisingly, many of Antony's generals and troops also decide to flee—straight to the side of Octavius. Loyal Enobarbus stays with his leader, although everything tells him he is a fool to do so.

It is not long before a full understanding of what he has done catches up with Antony. He begs his remaining friends to make their peace with Rome and hints that there is now only one way open to him. Cleopatra tries to comfort him, explaining that she had no idea he would follow her from the battle. Antony admits that his real conqueror is not Octavius Caesar but his love for the Egyptian queen.

Antony and Cleopatra send messages to Octavius. Antony asks only for his life and to be allowed to live in Egypt, or at least in Athens as a private citizen. Cleopatra asks only that her children can still follow her on the throne. Ceasar's reply is swift:

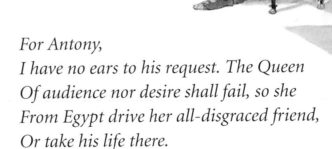

For Antony,
I have no ears to his request. The Queen
Of audience nor desire shall fail, so she
From Egypt drive her all-disgraced friend,
Or take his life there.

Antony's response is to challenge Octavius to single combat, but even he surely cannot think that the statesman Caesar will risk everything in an unequal battle against a skilled swordsman. Indeed, Caesar has more cunning plans. He sends messengers to try to flatter Cleopatra into betraying Antony.

Antony's misunderstanding of Cleopatra's response to Octavius almost causes a breach between them, but Cleopatra persuades him of her undiminished love and loyalty. Refuelled with courage, Antony determines to fight Caesar to the end.

> *I will be treble-sinewed, hearted, breath'd,*
> *And fight maliciously; … Come,*
> *Let's have one other gaudy night. Call to me*
> *All my sad captains; fill our bowls once more;*
> *Let's mock the midnight bell.*

While Antony and Cleopatra try to act as though all will be well, Octavius is steely and clear-thinking.

> *Let our best heads*
> *Know that to-morrow the last of many battles*
> *We mean to fight.*

As Antony takes his leave of Cleopatra the next morning, both of them know that they may never meet again. Even before the battle, Antony suffers a mighty blow when he hears that Enobarbus has deserted him. Showing his great-heartedness to the last, Antony sends Enobarbus' share of their spoils after him.

The arrival of the treasure from Antony is too much for Enobarbus.

> *I am alone the villain of the earth,*
> *And feel I am so most. O Antony…*
> *I will go seek*
> *Some ditch wherein to die…*

The first day of fighting is by land, where Antony's skill lies. His army is triumphant. In hopeful mood, Antony and Cleopatra celebrate with their generals. But the following day, the collapse of Antony's navy is fast and devastating.

In horror at what he sees and hears, Antony blames Cleopatra, who flees from him in fear for her life. But even at this stage, the queen cannot help scheming to regain Antony's love.

> *To th'monument!*
> *Mardian, go tell him I have*
> * slain myself;*
> *Say, that the last I spoke was*
> * "Antony",*
> *And word it, prithee, piteously.*
> * Hence, Mardian,*
> *And bring me how he takes my*
> * death.*

Suicide *in the face of dishonour was thought to be a very Roman action. It was considered noble and courageous to take your own life in such circumstances.*

When he is told that Cleopatra is no more, all the fight goes out of Antony.

> *…the long day's task is done,*
> *And we must sleep.*

Thinking of all he has lost, Antony falls upon his sword, but finds himself fatally wounded, not dead. He learns that Cleopatra is still alive and asks to be taken to her.

As Antony dies in her arms, Cleopatra speaks of his greatness.

> *Noblest of men, woo't die?*
> *Hast thou no care of me? Shall I abide*
> *In this dull world, which in thy absence is*
> *No better than a sty? O, see, my women,*
> *The crown o' the earth doth melt. My lord!*
> *O, wither'd is the garland of the war…*
> *And there is nothing left remarkable*
> *Beneath the visiting moon.*

Hearing of Antony's death, even Caesar grieves, but his mind is also on practical matters. He orders that Cleopatra must be guarded to prevent her from following her lover's example.

When Octavius Ceasar comes face to face with Cleopatra, he treats her with respect, but the queen knows that she will be led through the streets of Rome as a captive, when Octavius makes his triumphant return. An asp is smuggled to her in a basket of figs. For Cleopatra, death comes swiftly.

Strangely, it is Caesar, the enemy of Antony and Cleopatra, who ensures that the lovers will be reunited in death.

She shall be buried by her
Antony;
No grave upon the earth shall
clip in it
A pair so famous.

An asp is a small venomous snake, found in North Africa and Arabia. It seems that Cleopatra was ready for this moment, having studied painless and foolproof ways of committing suicide.

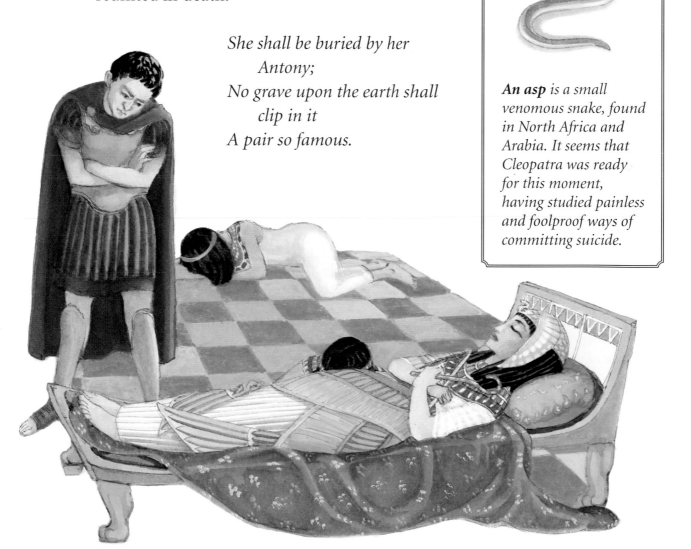

THE WORKS OF SHAKESPEARE

1590–1   *Henry VI, Parts 1, 2 and 3*

1592–3   *Richard III; The Comedy of Errors*

1593–4   *Titus Andronicus; The Taming of the Shrew*
                     Venus and Adonis; Lucrece

1593–1600 *Sonnets*

1594–5   *The Two Gentlemen of Verona; Love's Labour's Lost*
                     Romeo and Juliet

1595–6   *Richard II; A Midsummer Night's Dream*

1596–7   *King John; The Merchant of Venice*

1597–8   *Henry IV, Parts 1 and 2*

1598–1600 *Much Ado about Nothing; As You Like It;*
                     Twelfth Night; Henry V; Julius Caesar

1600–1   *Hamlet, Prince of Denmark;*
                     The Merry Wives of Windsor

1602   *Troilus and Cressida; All's Well that Ends Well*

1604–5   *Measure for Measure; Othello*

1605–6   *King Lear; Macbeth*

1606–7   *Antony and Cleopatra*

1607–8   *Coriolanus; Timon of Athens*

1609–11   *Pericles; Cymbeline; The Winter's Tale*

1611–12   *The Tempest*

1612–13   *Henry VIII; Two Noble Kinsmen*